MAKE EVERY
EARTH DAY

EcoBunny Adventure Club

"You aren't going to save the world on your own. But you might inspire a generation of kids to save it for all of us. You would be amazed at what inspired children can do."
Jane Goodall

"Young people - they care. They know that this is the world that they're going to grow up in, that they're going to spend the rest of their lives in. But, I think it's more idealistic than that. They actually believe that humanity, human species, has no right to destroy and despoil regardless."
Sir David Attenborough

HINT:

This story's special; here's a clue:
The adventure's path is chosen by one and only YOU!
YOU hold the power; YOU have a voice.
At each turn, YOU'll make a choice!
A journey of wonder where at every bend you'll see
The freedom to decide what the story will be.
Now turn the page, let's not delay,
EcoBunny's Earth Day is underway.
Choose wisely, have fun, and quickly you will see,
Just how your choices shape EcoBunny's journey!

In the heart of Paradise Cove,
Where the daisies sway,
Lives EcoBunny
Curious in every way.

"Earth Day's here,"
She says with a twirl,
"Let's make a difference,
Boys and girls!"

EcoBunny is playing
When she sees a river full of cans,
"What shall we do?
Let's come up with a plan!"

Option 1: Clean up the stream
With gloves and a song (Go to page 8)
Option 2: "It's just a few cans" she says,
And starts walking along… (Go to Page 10)

With some effort, a skip and a song, the stream's clean and bright,
EcoBunny says "Look at our work, what a delightful sight!"
Dolly Dolphin admires, "Thank you for helping me tidy up my home.
It's not just me that you're helping, but also others that roam.

Rivers can lead to lakes or the sea;
You're helping millions by keeping waterways clean!
Did you know, in just one day,
Our country throws 60 million plastic bottles away?
That's a lot of waste we can all reduce,
By choosing reusable bottles, we can put less to use!"
(Go to page 12)

As she hops along, the stream is killing flowers.
EcoBunny frowns, 'Oooooooooops , I underestimated its powers."
Deep down, she knows the right solution,
"We'll clean up all this human pollution!"

She returns with friends, to set things right,
"Let's fix our mistake, and use all our might."

10

Dolly Dolphin looks around,
"Oh this is much better, thank you for helping."
EcoBunny smiles, "Our efforts are jussssssst developing!

From murky to clear, our waters gleam bright,
Working together, we've made it all right.
Each day let's promise to keep our Earth neat,
For our beautiful home, and then we'll repeat
With every kind act, we show we are keen,
To care for our world, to keep it serene."
(Go to page 12)

11

Fixer Fox spots EcoBunny, looking quite down,
Next to a bicycle broken in the middle of town.

Daily, our broken things could fill trucks in a line
Reaching to the sky, maybe it's about time.
Instead of letting it all pile high,
Recycling and fixing is what we should try!

Option 1: Should he offer her aid,
    Join in and repair? (Go to page 14)
Option 2: Or walk on by,
    Pretending not to care? (Go to page 16)

Option 1

Fixing together, they laugh and chat,
"A problem shared is cut in half, just like that!"
"Teamwork and care," Fixer Fox beams with a smile,
"Can turn a big task into something worthwhile!
Fixing what's broken, even with a small fee,
Is less in the landfills, leaving more Earth to see.

New toys and things can lead to waste,
Let's use less, it's in good taste.
For our planet, let's be kind,
And leave less stuff behind!
When you can, try to fix or buy second hand,
It's a small notion but it helps the Motherland."
Fixer Fox continues, "Remember the 5 R's when you forget what to do,
Refuse, Reduce, Repurpose, Recycle and in this case REUSE (Go to page 20)

Option 2
Walking by,
EcoBunny ran into
a landfill and took a peek,
A mountain of stuff -
some new, some antique.
She saw the waste,
so vast and wide.
Her heart felt heavy;
she almost cried.

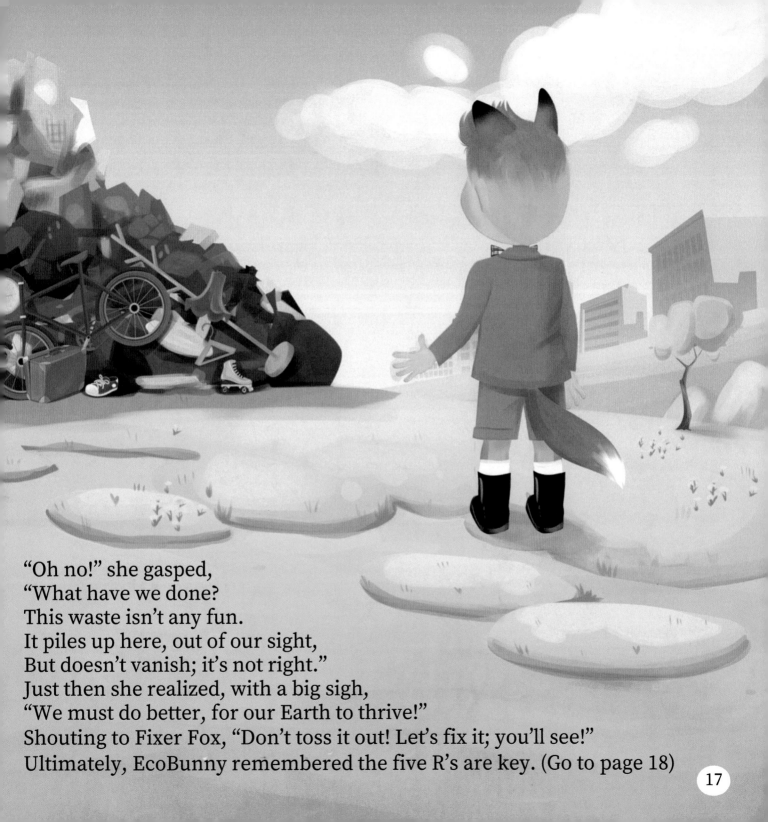

"Oh no!" she gasped,
"What have we done?
This waste isn't any fun.
It piles up here, out of our sight,
But doesn't vanish; it's not right."
Just then she realized, with a big sigh,
"We must do better, for our Earth to thrive!"
Shouting to Fixer Fox, "Don't toss it out! Let's fix it; you'll see!"
Ultimately, EcoBunny remembered the five R's are key. (Go to page 18)

1. Refuse what you don't need,
   Keep waste away,

2. Reduce what you use, make
   Less every day,

3. Reuse what you can, let's
   give things a new life,

4. Recycle what's old, to protect
   Earth and its wildlife.

5. A funny R is for Rot or
   Composting, if soil is it's fate.

The 5 R's help our planet, it's not too late!

MAKE OUR PLANET SMILE

With every R, they knew what to do,
Caring for the Earth, making her feel brand new.
(Go to page 20)

REFUSE

REDUCE

REUSE

RECYCLE

ROT

Next, EcoBunny finds trees marked to cut,
Should she put a stop to it – or- let them go kerplunk!

"Did you know," EcoBunny said with a frown,
"Every minute, forests are cut down?
That's like 40 football fields, gone in a blink,
What shall we do, let's stop and think!"

Let's plant seeds, lets spread the word,
For a healthier planet, let our voices be heard!"

Option 1: Rally to save the trees –
There's strength in numbers (Go to Page 22)
Option 2: Play under another tree
And maybe drift off to slumber (Go to Page 24)

Option 1
With banners and chants the trees stand tall,
"We can do it!" she shouts, "Let's save them all!"

YOUR PERSEVERANCE SAVES THE DAY,
EACH TREE IS STILL STANDING,
HIP HIP HOORAY!

Let's be sensible with paper,
Not waste, but treasure.
Recycle and reuse in equal measure.
(Go to page 26)

FRESH AIR

SAVE THE TREES!

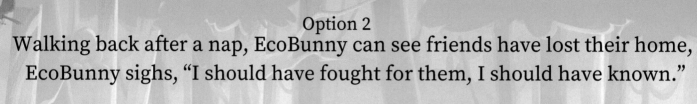

Walking back after a nap, EcoBunny can see friends have lost their home,
EcoBunny sighs, "I should have fought for them, I should have known."

She sees their sadness, feels their plight,
Knowing in her heart, it's time to do right.
Together they decide "Let's grow new homes and make amends,
Plant new trees; our lives depend on them...
A world lacking trees; oh what a mistake!
Let's cherish them all for our future's sake!" (Go to page 26)

Approaching a field of flowers,
Trampled and torn,
What should Blizzy do
In the early morn?

Option 1: Replant the flower seeds, they'll bloom and glow,
With sun and water, we can watch them grow. (Go to Page 28)
Option 2: Blizzy is way too busy, and has better things to do
Than to be worried about the birds' and butterflies' food. (Go to Page 30)

With seeds and care, the field's brand new,
"Beauty restored, thanks to our eco-warrior crew!"

Queenie Butterfly flutters. "This is where the smallest of creatures roam.

So thank you for saving
my beautiful home!"
(Go to Page 32)

All the bees lose their nectar, the field turns gray,
Blizzy realizes, "I should've replanted today."

Seeing the empty space, feeling the need,
Blizzy decides, "It's time to replant each and every seed."
Back they go, with seeds and cheer,
To bring back their homes; let's start here! (Go to Page 32)

Fixer Fox and Ryder Rhino ride to the shore,
Where they find plastic bottles and so much more.
Ryder knows this isn't an easy feat
While Fixer Fox would rather stop and eat.

Option 1: Ryder organizes a cleanup
With purpose and zest. (Go to Page 34)
Option 2: "Not my mess, "Fixer Fox jests, ,
Putting his love for nature to the test. (Go to Page 36)

With friends all around, Ryder Rhino cleans the shore,
Jokes and laughter, who could ask for more?

Myrtle the Green Turtle said, "You've made it so neat;
A clean beach for all, oh what a treat!"

34

"Remember," Ryder Rhino remarks with a smile so wide,
"Recycling helps more than just the beachside.
Instead of wasting or throwing stuff in our sea,
Recycling keeps waterways safe and free.
When we incorrectly toss things, it can end up here;
Let's make it our mission to make trash disappear!
Recycling right, as we all should,
Keeps our waters clean and that feels good. (Go to page 38)

Fixer Fox went walking, but spots Crabby with a plastic toy,
"I think we should help him, oh boy!"
His friends come help, with hands so small,
Together they pick up, for one and for all.

They clear the trash, both near and far,
Fixer Fox is feeling like a superstar!
"For every piece of junk we grab,
We are helping the planet AND Crabby Crab!

When we visit places, by foot or by car,
Let's leave them better than they are."
Pick up and tidy up as we play,
So nature's beauty shines every day."

Blizzy Bee is buzzing around the flowers, happy and free,
Sees a sick friend, uh-oh, could it be a pesticide spree?
Here's a fact, sad but true,
These chemicals can harm our sweet buzzing crew.

Every year, it's clear to see,
These chemicals hurt our buzzing bee.
With each spray, their numbers dip,
Making it hard on their flower trip.

Option 1: No more chemicals on our plant friends," Blizzy decides with a buzz.
I'll find a better way, that's what a good bee does!" (Go to Page 40)
Option 2: Blizzy sees the plants, covered in something sticky and new,
Feels unsure at first…is there anything he needs to do? (Go to Page 42)

Hearing Blizzy's words, EcoBunny jumps to aid,
"With our determination, there's no need to be afraid!"

Together they spread the word to all the nearby bees
"Let's keep our plants and air clean, pretty please?" (Go to page 44)

Initially hesitant, Blizzy Bee takes a moment, then flies high,
Seeing a family of sick bees, he lets out a big sigh.
Bees buzz around, from flower to flower,
Working hard, hour by hour.
Did you know, and this fact's quite peachy
One-third of our food comes from an itty bitty bee?
Fruits, veggies, and even some seeds
Depend on bees for their pollinating deeds.

Finding friends to help, they all start to think,
"Let's clean this mess, and make these chemicals shrink.
We should try to help in any way,
For bees to safely work and play." (Go to page 44)

As the sun sets, they wonder, "Can everyday be Earth Day,
What path shall we now choose?"

Option 1: If we skip what we've learned, it won't be much fun.
Let's think twice before this choice is done. (Go to page 46)
Option 2: Or is it time to embrace a fresh start,
And guard nature's treasures with all our hearts? (Go to page 48)

Thinking 'bout tomorrow, what if trees could frown?
We'd want to make them smile, not let them down.
What if rivers could whisper, telling us to care?
We'd clean their waters, show them we can be fair.

What if birds in skies sang a tune so sad?
We'd give them reasons to feel grateful and glad.
Imagine if the Earth could laugh, be cheerful and bright,
We'd work to keep her joyful, morning to night.

"Let's not wait," they decide with a new plan,
"To make every day better, yes we can!"

So, they promise to balance fun with care
For our beautiful Earth, so precious, beyond compare.
A lesson to learn from their itty bitty mistakes,
To giving back to Earth, for everyone's sake. (Go to page 50)

Option 2

As EcoBunny rests, under a moon so clear,
She reflects on their journey, far and near.
"Every action we choose sends ripples through the land,
In caring for our Earth, together we stand."

"Cleaning our oceans and safeguarding fields and trees,
Brings health to our world, not just the birds and the bees.
Even small deeds, like using less,
Makes our world better - a real success!" (Go to Page 50)

As the night falls on our EcoBunny's quest,
Her heart's full of joy; she's done her best!
From rivers cleaned to flowers anew,
With every step she took, Earth's beauty grew.
With friends by her side, and courage so bright,
They showed the world how to do things right.

"Make Every Day Earth Day!" they cheer with delight,
For a greener tomorrow, we'll all unite."
So, let's hop along with EcoBunny's band,
Caring for our Earth, hand in hand.
Adventure awaits, in your own backyard,
Let's all protect the planet, it isn't hard!

ANIMALS BEHIND THE CHARACTERS
ARE ON THE ENDANGERED SPECIES LIST

SUMATRAN TIGER (TINY TIGER)

ANDRENA MINER BEE (BUZZY BEE)

COLUMBIA BASIN PYGMY RABBIT (ECOBUNNY)

MONARCH BUTTERFLY (QUEENIE)

AMAZON RIVER DOLPHIN (DOLLY DOLPHIN)

SIERRA NEVADA RED FOX (FIXER FOX)

SOUTHERN RIVER OTTER

BLACK RHINO (RYDER RHINO)

GREEN TURTLE (MYRTLE TURTLE)

SEEING DOUBLE

We explore two distinct sets of 5R's, both essential to our planet's well-being.

1 The 1st set includes Refuse, Reduce, Repurpose, Recycle, and Reuse. This sequence emphasizes the importance of saying no to unnecessary items, minimizing waste, creatively reusing materials, recycling what we can't reuse, and repurposing items to extend their lifecycle.

2 The 2nd set shifts slightly to introduce Rot, replacing Repurpose, and giving us Refuse, Reduce, Reuse, Recycle, and Rot. Here, the focus is on composting organic waste (Rot), which enriches the soil and reduces methane emissions from landfills.

Both sets of R's guide our journey towards sustainability, reflecting the multifaceted approach required to protect our Earth.

FACTS

Page 9 Americans throw 60 million plastic bottles away every day, according to the Container Recycling Institute. Reducing single-use plastic protects our rivers, lakes and oceans.

Page 12 The average U.S. person generates 4.9lbs of trash/day - EPA circa 2023. With a population of over 330 million, that's more than 1.6 billion lbs of trash/day.

Page 20 World Wildlife Fund reports that up to 48 football field's worth of forests are lost every minute due to deforestation. The United Nation's Food and Agriculture Organization (FAO) and other environmental organizations highlight that animal agriculture is a major factor in deforestation. This involves clearing forests to create land for grazing livestock and growing crops to feed animals that are for human consumption.

Page 38 + 39 Environmental Protection Agency (EPA) acknowledges the negative impact and decline of bees due to pesticides. The Food and Agriculture Organization of the United Nations (FAO) highlights the crucial role of bees and other pollinators in contributing to food security, with one-third of the world's crop production depending on these insects. Furthermore, the Center for Biological Diversity concluded that pesticides can turn healthy soil into a not so happy home for fruit, vegetables and other plants.